S0-FBD-150

To Pat
Breathe

BREATHE, GABBY, BREATHE!

Copyright 2023 by Paula Johnson Neal. All rights reserved. No part of this publication may be reproduced, distributed, or transmitted in any form or by any means, including photocopying, recording, other electronic or mechanical methods, without the prior written permission of the publisher, except in the case of brief quotations embodied in critical reviews and certain other noncommercial uses permitted by copyright law. For permission requests, please contact Paula Johnson Neal at PJN.BOOKS4@GMAIL.COM   PJN BOOKS Columbus, Ohio www.PaulaJohnsonNeal.com
ISBN: 979-8-988 183600

I dedicate this book to little Paula for reminding me of my childhood dreams. Thank you to my mom, Pearlie, and siblings, Vernell, Deborah, Jackie, James, Kathy, Sheila, and Sharon."

IT'S MORNING.

Gabby sat up in bed, yawning while stretching her arms. Then, after wiping the sleep from her eyes, Gabby let out a loud, "WHAT?"

All of her toys, television, and games were gone! Gabby yelled.

"MOMMY! DADDY!"

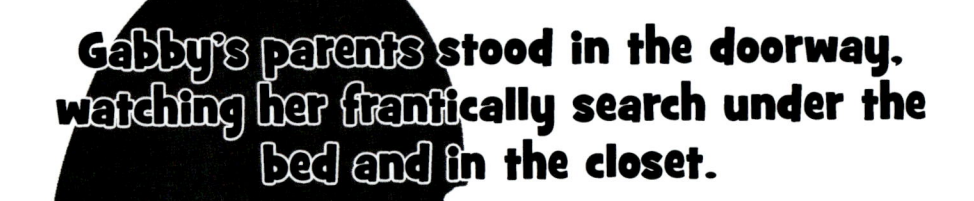

Gabby's parents stood in the doorway, watching her frantically search under the bed and in the closet.

"WHERE ARE MY TOYS?" whispered Gabby.

"We have decided to take away your toys. Yesterday, you did not have a good day at school. You must make good choices by showing kindness to your friends," responded her dad.

"I'm going to have a good day at school," said Gabby!

"You have said that many times before. You will earn your toys back by having better days. How are you going to have better days?" asked her dad.

"Ah, I'm going to use nice words, share, and wait my turn," replied Gabby.

"How will you make sure not to hurt your classmates?" questioned her dad.

"Um, I'm not going to pull anyone's chair," said Gabby.

"You will also apologize to Mrs. Beetle and your entire class," said her mom.

"Ok, mommy! Can we get ice cream after school?" Gabby excitedly requested.

"No." replied her parents.

Gabby peeked around the corner into the classroom as Mrs. Beetle greeted her parents.

"Good morning, Mrs. Beetle. I'm going to have a good day," stated Gabby.

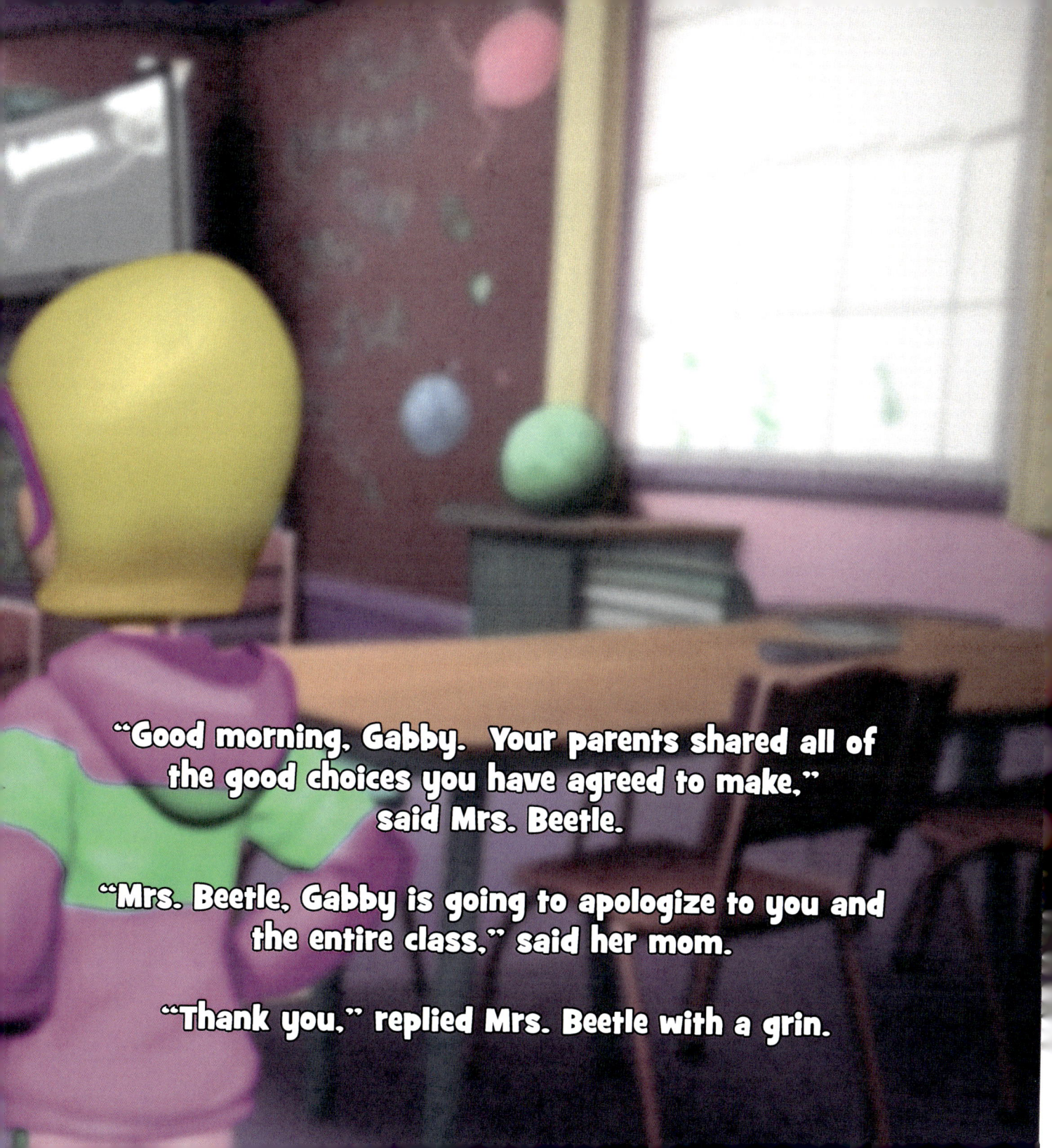

"Good morning, Gabby. Your parents shared all of the good choices you have agreed to make," said Mrs. Beetle.

"Mrs. Beetle, Gabby is going to apologize to you and the entire class," said her mom.

"Thank you," replied Mrs. Beetle with a grin.

"Gabby, please help me gather your classmates for circle time," requested Mrs. Beetle.

RING! RING!

Gabby rang the bell for circle time as the class gathered onto the carpet.

"Friends, yesterday Gabby struggled with making good choices. She would like to speak with you this morning," announced Mrs. Beetle.

Gabby held her head down as she apologized. "I'm sorry I called you names. I'm sorry I hurt you, Sophia. I'm going to have a good day."

All of her classmates continued to sit quietly until Max yelled, "No, you're not!"

"Am too!" said Gabby.

"You always say that, Gabby. I'm not your friend!" cried Sophia.

Mrs. Beetle said, "We all make mistakes. Let's give our friend Gabby another chance to use nice words and soft touches."

"She's always screaming. It hurts our ears. Gabby, you need to breathe," said Max.

"Let's all breathe," noted Mrs. Beetle.

Mrs. Beetle quietly instructed the class, "Sit crisscross applesauce, hands on knees, eyes closed. Now INHALE, exhale, INHALE, and exhale. Let's do it one more time. Eyes closed, INHALE, exhale, INHALE, and exhale. Better?"

All of the children chimed, "Yes."

Mrs. Beetle softly stated, "Gabby, thank you for your apology. Please remember to breathe and make good choices. If you need me, I will be close by."

Gabby struggled with making good choices throughout the day. She yelled, "I'm Gonna Have A Good Day," when not allowed to be unkind to her friends during play.

Mrs. Beetle continued to calm Gabby down by helping her to breathe.

During outdoor play, Gabby watched a group of children playing a game of "Duck, Duck, Goose!"

"I WANT TO.....," Gabby paused, looked over at Mrs. Beetle, and decided to ask the children with nicer words.

"May I play?" asked Gabby.
"Yes," replied the children.
"It's my turn. I'm the Ducker," said Gabby.

"No, I'm the Ducker. You need to wait your turn," said Layla.
Gabby impatiently shouted "Pick ME! I'm the GOOSE!"
Layla picked a different friend.

Gabby became upset, closed her eyes, and tried to yell
"I'M GONNA...I'M GONNA...."
But, only loud screeching sounds came from her mouth.
The children burst into laughter.

Gabby peeked from one eye and burst into laughter, too. "Breathe, Gabby, Breathe! YOU CAN DO IT!" said the children. Gabby closed her eyes as she INHALED, exhaled, INHALED, and exhaled. She opened her eyes, smiled, and said "Better."

Mrs. Beetle walked over to Gabby and gave her the biggest hug.
"Gabby, you made a really good choice. Are you proud of yourself?"
Gabby shook her head, "Yes."

Gabby asked, "Mrs. Beetle, are you going to tell my mommy and daddy I had a good day?"
Mrs. Beetle replied, "I'm going to inform your parents you had a better day."

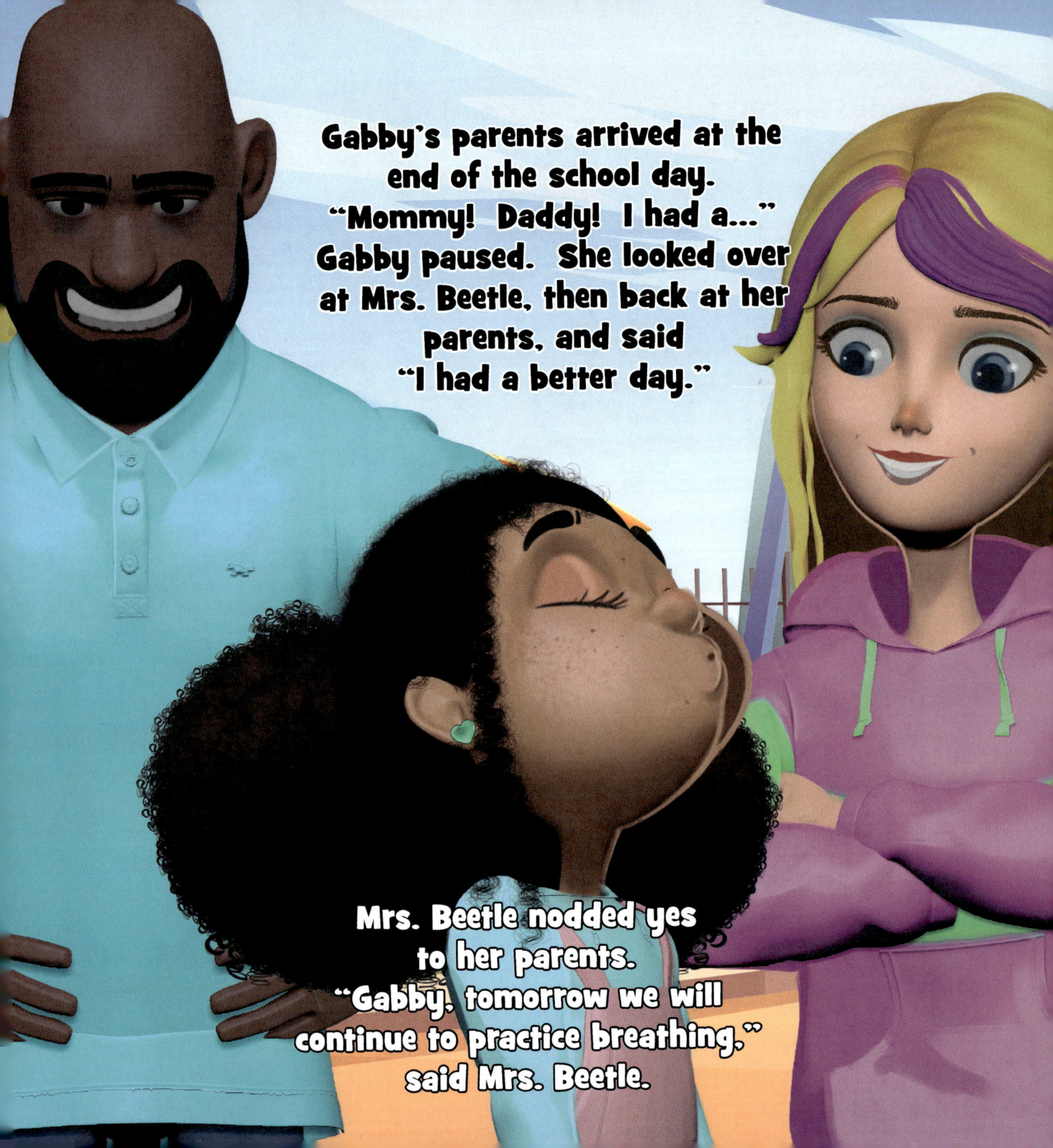

Gabby's parents arrived at the end of the school day. "Mommy! Daddy! I had a..." Gabby paused. She looked over at Mrs. Beetle, then back at her parents, and said "I had a better day."

Mrs. Beetle nodded yes to her parents. "Gabby, tomorrow we will continue to practice breathing," said Mrs. Beetle.

Gabby smiled as she playfully inhaled too much air, causing Mrs. Beetle and her parents to laugh while cheering,

"BREATHE, GABBY, BREATHE!"

About the Author:

Paula Johnson Neal is an award winner of the 2021 SVFC Corcoran Award for her first children's book, I'm Gonna Have A Good Day. Paula is a graduate of The Ohio State University with a degree in early childhood development. She resides in Columbus, Ohio, and enjoys spending time with family, friends, zip-lining, indoor skydiving, people-watching, and traveling. Paula, an avid reader since childhood, grew up with limited and poor representations of black children in storybooks. Paula writes for all children. However, she understands the necessity for quality representation and unlimited children's books with black characters as the lead protagonist.

- www.PaulaJohnsonNeal.com
- instagram.com/paulajohnsonneal
- facebook.com/paulajohnsonneal/
- PJN.Books4@gmail.com
- @paulajohnsonneal4414
- PaulaJohnsonNeal

About The Illustrator:

Tyrus Goshay is an award-winning digital illustrator and 3D artist with over 18 years of experience. He is a college professor, teaching game design and illustration in his off time. Tyrus has a Bachelor in Computer Animation and Multimedia and a Master's degree in Teaching With Technology (MALT). He has contributed to several award-winning projects in the world of toy design, and has been recognized for his achievements in academia. Tyrus became a certified speaker with Eric Thomas's "E.T. The Hip-hop Preacher" and Associates Game Changers Program in 2022. He has begun touring schools across the country, encouraging students and educators to tap into their creative potential. Are you looking to share your story by creating your book? Reach out to Tyrus@

- Youtube.com/TheCyruse4
- facebook.com/tgosketch
- Admin@tgosketch.com
- Instagram.com/tgosketch
- tgosketch
- www.tgosketch.com

Made in the USA
Middletown, DE
30 August 2023